IGNITING YOUR DAY

31 Days of Declarations
To Ignite the Power Of God's
Word In Your Life

Pastors Joe and Bella Garcia

Igniting Your Day

Copyright © 2017 Joe & Bella Garcia

All rights reserved.

ISBN-13: 978-1978103368

All Rights Reserved. No part of this publication may be reproduced, stored in a retrieval system or transmitted in any form or by any means – online, electronic, mechanical, photocopy, recording or any other – except for brief quotations in printed reviews, without prior permission of the author.

All Scripture quotations, unless otherwise specified, are from the King James Version of the Bible (Copyright © 1977, 1984, Thomas Nelson Inc., Publishers.)

Job 22:28
You shall also decree a thing, and it shall be established for you:
and the light shall shine upon your ways.

DEDICATION

We would like to dedicate this book to our three children: Andrew, Joel and Rachel Garcia. We are so very proud of who you are. Thanks for being you and for loving Jesus the way you do. We can't wait to see where God takes you and the many lives you will touch and empower with your unique gifts as you continue to ignite the Word of God in your lives each day. We love you and are very honored to be your parents.

TABLE OF CONTENTS

- DAY 1 -

DECLARING GOD'S WORD

God's desire is to have a relationship with you, to bless you so you can be a blessing.

The blessings in His Word are yours as you believe, receive, and endeavor to follow His commandments.

He wants you to live in the fullness of His Word and manifest power of His glorious presence.

Today, as you read and activate His Word by declaring that the truths are yours, the Heavenly realms are being opened over your life, your possessions, your loved ones, your circumstances and everything you represent.

Partner with His Word today, believe the Word on purpose and speak the Word with power.

There is life and power in His Word when you declare and decree a thing.

When you agree with God's Word, you are agreeing with Him.

Numbers 23:19

God is not man, that He should lie, or a son of man, that He should change His mind. Has He said, and will He not do it? Or has He spoken, and will He not fulfill it?

Psalm 119:130

The unfolding of your words gives light; it gives understanding to the simple.

Isaiah 40:8

The grass withers and the flowers fall, but the Word of our God endures forever.

Matthew 7:24

Therefore everyone who hears these words of mine and puts them into practice is like a wise man who built his house on the rock.

Luke 11:28

He replied, "Blessed rather are those who hear the Word of God and obey it."

Declaration

Thank You for Your Word, Lord; I know it is powerful, alive and will activate all You have promised me as I obey Your instructions and partner with You.

I cherish Your Word above all I possess because it is You speaking to me.

I declare the promises in Your Word are for me as well as my household.

Your Word is all that matters, the bottom line to every question or situation I will ever face.

I will know and hear Your voice by spending time reading Your Word.

I receive Your wisdom, love, peace, instructions and life that is in Your Word.

You love communicating with me so much that You called Jesus, my Savior, "The Word".

- DAY 2 -

YOU CAN DO IT

As you are preparing to face your day, remember this... YOU CAN DO IT.

The challenges may be great; maybe the mountains ahead of you are very high and the valleys before you seem very low ... maybe you feel like you are crossing a desert, but remember this... YOU CAN DO IT.

Or maybe today things are going well for you and there is an acceleration in your life, and the favor of the Lord is catapulting you into greater things. Still, remember this... YOU CAN DO IT.

Whatever you are facing today, the lows or the highs, remember... YOU CAN DO IT.

God will be with you every step of the way. You are not alone; He is here to help and guide you so YOU

CAN DO IT.

He will give you the strength, wisdom, and power to fulfill His purpose today.

Never stop looking up and remember to give Him all the glory!

Isaiah 41:10

Do not fear [anything], for I am with you; do not be afraid, for I am your God. I will strengthen you, be assured I will help you. I will certainly take hold of you with My righteous right hand [a hand of justice, of power, of victory, of salvation].

Philippians 4:13

I can do all things [which He has called me to do] through Him who strengthens and empowers me *to fulfill His purpose—I am self-sufficient in Christ's sufficiency; I am ready for anything and equal to anything through Him who infuses me with inner strength and confident peace.*

Declaration

Thank You, Lord, for You are with me.

I declare today that "I CAN DO IT" and that I am not alone.

I thank You for Your Word that says I can do all things that You have planned.

Thank You for Your strength, Your wisdom, and Your ability to do all that I must do today.

With You, I can face anything today.

Your Word says that You ordain my steps and Your presence is with me.

Thank You, Holy Spirit, for being right here with me.

I invite You right now to partner with me so You can lead me through anything and everything that I might face today.

Today, tomorrow, and every day, I will remember that I CAN DO IT with Your help, Lord, and I will always give You the glory.

- DAY 3 -

OVERCOMERS ARE ON THE WINNING TEAM

Your first plan of action to overcoming is partnering with God because with God on your side you will always succeed.

If you're wondering how you will get through this difficult time, just remember that God has equipped you to be an overcomer.

You have what it takes to win; you have the power of God living inside you.

Whatever the challenges may be, God has the victory all planned out.

Faith is the victory that overcomes the world.

Focus on God's power and plan rather than on the size of the problem.

Trust in God's plan for a victorious outcome even when it doesn't make sense.

See the supernatural in all situations and you will see the victory in the natural.

You don't need the removal of an affliction as much as you need the wisdom of God to overcome.

He makes molehills out of mountains.

Overcomers win every time.

Isaiah 54:17

No weapon that is formed against you shall prosper; and every tongue that shall rise against you in judgment you shall condemn. This is the heritage of the servants of the Lord, and their righteousness is of Me, says the Lord.

John 16:33

I have told you these things, so that in Me you may have peace. In this world you will have trouble. But take heart! I have overcome the world.

2 Corinthians 4:17

For our light and temporary affliction is producing for us an eternal glory that far outweighs our troubles.

James 1:12

Blessed is the man who perseveres under trial, because when he has stood the test, he will receive the crown of life that God has promised to those who love Him.

<u>Declaration</u>

I declare I have the overcoming power of God dwelling on the inside of me.

I have Jesus the Victory who overcame the world and who will never leave me.

I decree the power and protection of God go with me to push me to the finish line.

God has already won every battle for me and I declare I will always be the victor and never again the victim.

I declare that God is on my side and I am on His team; with Him all things are always possible.

- DAY 4 -

HE IS YOUR COMFORTER

The Word says Jesus was moved with compassion.

He is the same yesterday, today, and forever; He is still moved with compassion to pour out on you the Spirit without measure to comfort you today.

You can receive this compassion and comfort from a loving, compassionate God.

The work of the Holy Spirit is not only your Comforter but also your Counselor, Helper, Teacher, Advocate, Intercessor, Strengthener, and Standby.

You are His beloved and He is yours.

You are being supernaturally trained to be led by the Spirit of God and not led by your feelings or emotions.

Isaiah 40:1

"Comfort, comfort My people," says your God.

Isaiah 49:13

Shout for joy, O heavens! And rejoice, O earth! Break forth into joyful shouting, O mountains! For the Lord has comforted His people And will have compassion on His afflicted.

John 14:16

And I will pray the Father, and He shall give you another Comforter, that He may abide with you forever.

Acts 2:38

Repent, and be baptized every one of you in the name of Jesus Christ for the remission of sins, and ye shall receive the gift of the Holy Ghost.

Declaration

Thank You, Lord, for the Comforter You gave me.

I declare the comfort and power of the Holy Spirit dwell in me and I am filled to overflowing with His supernatural strength today.

Everything that Jesus was I decree I also have through the Spirit who abides in me.

I am more than a conqueror when I am focused on the power of God.

I decree today I will never be without my Helper, my Wisdom, and my Comforter.

I give You all the praise and thanksgiving for the power of the Holy Spirit who comforts me and gives me peace in every storm.

- DAY 5 -

YOU WILL ARISE AND SHINE

Arise from the place where you have been.

See yourself arising from the place where circumstances have kept you.

You are not defined by your circumstances, and you are not defined by your past.

Arise to a new life, and let the glory of the Lord radiate through you.

Everything that the Glory touches will change.

Let the Glory of the Lord touch you today and infuse your circumstances with light.

Light cancels out darkness every time.

For His light is shining in every dark area of your life today; everything is coming alive because of the Light of the Lord.

Proverbs 4:18

The way of the righteous is like the first gleam of dawn, which shines ever brighter until the full light of day.

Isaiah 60:1

Arise, shine; for your light has come, and the glory of the Lord is risen upon you.

Luke 11:36

Therefore, if your whole body is full of light, and no part of it dark, it will be just as full of light as when a lamp shines its light on you.

Ephesians 5:8

For you were once darkness, but now you are light in the Lord. Live as children of light.

Declaration

Thank You for Your light, Lord.

You are the light of the world and I receive that light so I can share it with the world.

I choose to arise and shine, so I am arising in You today.

I am a child of the light.

I thank You that Your light is shining bright and everything is coming alive in me today.

I thank You that I›m not defined by the darkness that used to surround the circumstances of my past.

Your Word is causing the light to shine brighter and brighter in me today.

Your light dispels every bit of darkness trying to stop me.

Thank You that Your Glory is changing me and my circumstances today.

I am being renewed and refreshed today as I arise and shine, in Jesus' name.

- DAY 6 -

OPEN DOORS

The door that God opens will never contradict His Word.

The door that God opens will be accompanied by supernatural confirmation and peace.

The door that God opens will require you to depend on Him to walk through.

Every open door is a God-given opportunity for you to help advance His Kingdom.

As you love the Lord and endeavor to obey His Word, God has many open doors of opportunities ahead for you.

You limit your ministry or business success when you force open doors of your choosing; remember your life belongs to God.

Jesus is the Door of Opportunity and He says it is always open; so keep watching, walking, listening, expecting and praising Him.

Don't try to re-open doors that God already told you to close.

When you know the voice of the Father and respond to Him, the door will open and you'll walk through.

Isaiah 22:22

Then I will set the key of the house of David on His shoulder, when He opens no one will shut, when He shuts no one will open.

John 10:9

I am the Door. If anyone enters by Me, he will be saved and will go in and out and find pasture.

Revelation 4:1

After this I looked, and behold, [a]a door standing open in heaven! And the first voice which I had heard, like the sound of a [war] trumpet speaking with me, said, "Come up here, and I will show you what must take place after these things."

Declaration

Thank You, Father, that You are my Door that is always open for me.

Your doors are the only ones that I want to walk through, Lord.

I decree new doors are coming into focus today.

I decree there is always a way that is open to me.

Help me never to force doors to open that You want to keep shut.

I will keep walking, listening, and expecting new doors to spring forth in Your timing, Lord.

Your doors will not be shut by anyone who tries to stop me.

I declare the right door will open at the right time, every time ... in Jesus' name.

THE FAVOR AND MERCY OF GOD

Recognize that it's not by luck or by chance; it's the intentional Favor of God.

He delights in showing favor and mercy to His children, and He wants you to have every benefit and walk in every promise.

One act of kindness can unlock a lifetime of favor.

Truth without mercy becomes callused, hard, cold and legalistic.

Favor promotes and protects you and will even cause your enemies to be at peace with you.

Jesus grew in favor both socially and spiritually. (Luke 2:52)

Divine favor draws unbelievers to Christians as well as to Christ.

Never stay where there is an absence of favor.

Genesis 39:4

Joseph found favor in his sight and became his personal servant; and he made him overseer over his house, and all that he owned he put in his charge.

Psalm 5:12

For You, O LORD, bless the righteous man [the one who is in right standing with You]. You surround him with Favor as with a shield.

Psalm 103:4, 11, 17

Who redeems your life from destruction, who crowns you with lovingkindness and tender mercies... the heavens are high above the earth so great is His Mercy to those who fear Him. The mercy of the Lord is from everlasting to everlasting on those who fear Him.

Luke 2:52

And Jesus increased in wisdom and stature, and in Favor with God and man.

Declaration

I declare Your mercy will strengthen me with grace and forgiveness.

Nothing is too difficult for You, Lord, so I receive your favor and mercy right now.

I believe Your Word that assures me Your mercy is brand new every morning and from everlasting to everlasting.

Your favor will sustain me, bless me and then become a great blessing to everyone I meet.

I can do all things with Your love, favor, and mercy surrounding me.

I praise You continuously for all the benefits of the cross and resurrection; new life in Jesus has brought imminent favor and mercy.

HIS LOVE NEVER FAILS

His unconditional love is always available to you.

God loves you and there is nothing you can do to change that.

No matter what you have done, or what you will do, His love for you will never change.

Even though you might fail Him, His love never fails you.

Love builds and heals people; it's the greatest force in the universe.

You will never be wrong when you walk in love.

The power of God's love is contagious and motivating.

His unfailing love is limitless and will always be available for any need you have.

His love for you was the reason behind sacrificing His Son on your behalf.

You have been set free because of love.

If you have God, you have love.

Psalm 100:5

For the Lord is good, His lovingkindness is ever-lasting and His faithfulness to all generations.

John 5:13

Greater love has no man than this that he lay down his life for his friends.

1 Corinthians 13:4-8

Love is patient, love is kind. It does not envy, it does not boast, it is not proud. It does not dishonor others, it is not self-seeking, it is not easily angered, it keeps no record of wrongs. Love does not delight in evil but rejoices with the truth. It always protects, always trusts, always hopes, always perseveres. Love never fails. But where there are prophecies, they will cease; where there are tongues, they will be stilled; where there is knowledge, it will pass away.

<u>Declaration</u>

I receive Your unconditional love without measure.

I am thankful for the amazing love You extend to me.

I declare I am forgiven for not believing the truth about who You are and how much You really do love me.

I pray for a life-transforming revelation of Your affection for me so I might relate to You and to others in a fresh, new, loving way.

I decree that as I choose to let go of the past I will begin to love myself as You love me.

Teach and help me to love like You, Lord.

- DAY 9 -

HIS SECRET RESTING PLACE OF PEACE

God has given you authority over every storm that tries to rage against you.

You have full and complete authority to speak to any chaos in your life and say, "Peace, be still!"

In the midst of every trial, there is a place where you can hide, be safe, rest and receive supernatural peace.

Hiding in the Lord is like being in the eye of a storm, in the center of His will, and in the Secret Place.

Today you can exchange stress for peace.

To rest in the Lord is to believe that He can help you, save you, and deliver you in your most urgent, chaotic or stressful need.

When you truly believe, then you can truly trust, and therefore, you can truly receive rest.

There is a time to be still, quiet and peaceful while you are being refueled for the next part of the journey; follow the Lord.

Psalm 29:11

The Lord will give strength to His people; The Lord will bless His people with peace.

Matthew 11:28-30

Come to Me, all who labor and are heavy laden, and I will give you rest. Take My yoke upon you, and learn from Me, for I am gentle and lowly in heart, and you will find rest for your souls. For My yoke is easy, and My burden is light.

2 Thessalonians 3:16

Now may the Lord of peace Himself give you peace at all times and in every way. The Lord be with all of you.

<u>Declaration</u>

I declare the Word of the Lord over my life today and I receive peace, rest, and quietness.

I hear His Word, trust in it, and declare my family enters His rest; the Secret Place is the place where we want to abide forever.

When illness, suffering, difficulties, anguish, confusion, fear, weakness or worry try to overwhelm me, I will remember to rest and trust in His Word.

Your Word enlightens me, strengthens and comforts me and gives me peace.

I decree that Your yoke is easy so when I am feeling heavy, I will rest in Your Word that gives me the peace of God that passes all earthly understanding.

I receive the vocabulary of a peacemaker and everywhere I walk and speak people will receive of the same.

- DAY 10 -

HE RESTORES ALL

Redemption and restoration are the work of God through His Son, Jesus Christ.

God can totally restore all that you have lost if you trust and allow Him to do it.

Money can be restored, a property can be restored, and relationships can all be restored.

God can restore painful, fruitless, Christ-less, penniless, selfish, wasted or rebellious years; nothing is too difficult for Him if you let Him.

Restoration and redemption cannot be reversed; it was finished on the cross.

It was too precious and costly a thing for God to make restoration dependent on you.

The deep depths of the heavy cost of your redemption ensure that it is entirely in God's hands.

God can restore lost years by bringing long-term gain from a short-term loss.

He redeemed you. You belong to him. Every curse is completely broken.

Joel 2:25

I will restore the years that the locust has eaten.

Psalm 23:3

He restores my soul: He leads me in the paths of righteousness for His name's sake.

Acts 1:6-7

Then they gathered around Him and asked Him, "Lord, are you at this time going to restore the kingdom to Israel?" He said to them, "It is not for you to know times or seasons that the Father has fixed by His own authority."

Declaration

I declare the supernatural restoration of the Lord belongs to me right now.

I trust You, Jesus, to restore everything that appears to be lost, stolen, broken or irreplaceable.

I believe You are bringing those family members who are wandering from Your path home once again.

I know You can reverse the clock and restore the years that appear to be lost or wasted.

I believe You can bring peace and faith in the restoration of all things that are precious to me.

Nothing is too difficult for You, Father.

I agree with You and decree it is done, in Jesus' mighty name.

- DAY 11 -

THE FAMILY OF GOD

God created your physical family and your spiritual family.

Refuse to allow rebellion and strife in your home or in your circle of influence.

The family is the very foundation of every society.

God places great value on the family and great value on leadership and authority in the home; Divine authority creates Divine order.

Parents are to teach by example: to protect, provide, love, honor, and respect each other and the children.

The family is the place where children learn to grow, forgive, listen, obey and be responsible.

Your home is your own responsibility, the master garden of your life; 'pull weeds' and 'plant flowers' to create the fragrance and atmosphere of Heaven.

The body of Christ is your family and He places single people in Godly families.

Genesis 1:27-28

So God created man in His own image, in the image of God created He him; male and female created He them. And God blessed them, and God said unto them, be fruitful, and multiply, and fill the earth, and subdue it: and have dominion over the fish of the sea, and over the fowl of the air, and over every living thing that moves upon the earth.

Psalm 127:3

Behold, children are a gift of the Lord, the fruit of the womb is a reward.

Romans 12:5

So we, being many, are one body in Christ, and every one members one of another.

Declaration

I am thankful for my family, Lord, for the spouse, children, and spiritual family You have given me to care for and encourage.

Help me to be a Godly, responsible example to everyone in my sphere of influence.

I declare I am more like Jesus today because of Your Word that transforms me.

As I pursue You today, impart the Wisdom of Heaven and great understanding and patience where I need it the most.

I desire to raise up powerful men and women for You, Lord.

Give me an immeasurable, unconditional and supernatural love for my physical children and spiritual children; may they see Jesus in me at all times.

I give You praise and thanksgiving for teaching me to be a leader in the Body of Christ.

ALL YOUR NEEDS ARE MET

Believe and trust that today God has provided for and supplied all your needs.

There is nothing too small or too big that God has not already made provision for.

You are in Him and He is in you; He is more than enough for you.

God promises to supply not some, but ALL of your needs.

He created you to live in abundance and He takes pleasure in your prosperity.

God knows what you will need today, before you may even realize.

When situations arise that look like lack, just remember that His provision will be there and you will always have more than enough.

Agree with Heaven today; when you agree with Heaven, all of Heaven agrees with you.

Genesis 39:6

So Potiphar left everything he had in Joseph's care; with Joseph in charge, he did not concern himself with anything except the food he ate.

Philippians 4:19

And God is able to make all grace abound to you, so that in all things, at all times, having all that you need, you will abound in every good work.

Matthew 6:8

Be not therefore like them: for your Father knows what things you have need of, before you ask Him.

Mark 10:30

But he shall receive a hundredfold now in this time, houses, and brothers, and sisters, and mothers, and children, and lands, with persecutions; and in the world to come eternal life.

Declaration

Thank You for Your promises in Your Word, Lord; there is nothing You have not provided for me.

I declare all my needs are already met because of Jesus.

Everything You have ordained me to do is provided for already and I have nothing to worry about.

Everywhere You designed for me to go, I will get there with Your provision, Your power, and Your plan.

I decree You have not left me alone to figure out how to do anything; You are there with Your hands opened and with plenty of provisions.

I praise You right now, Father God, for everything that I need is found in You.

YOU WILL NOT QUIT

Don't give up today for you are always on the brink of another miracle.

When you choose not to give up, you are saying God is able; when you quit, you're saying it was too difficult for God!

Believe that He is more than able to help you through every circumstance.

God is always going to see you through to the answer you need.

Focus on His promises and don't quit; stay the course and you will surely cross over.

You are not a quitter because Jesus never gave up, gave in or quit when the going got tough.

He is your ever-present help and example in times of trouble.

God will turn your obstacles into roads, highways, and paths if you do not quit.

Isaiah 40:28

Have you not known? Have you not heard? The Lord is the everlasting God, the Creator of the ends of the earth. He does not faint or grow weary; His understanding is unsearchable.

Isaiah 40:31

Yet those who wait for the Lord will gain new strength; they will mount up with wings like eagles, they will run and not get tired, they will walk and not become weary.

2 Thessalonians 3:13

But as for you, brethren, do not grow weary of doing good.

Declaration

I declare I will not lose heart, faint or become weary in doing good today.

You are my example, Jesus, and You will give me supernatural perseverance to finish my race.

I decree I am a finisher, not a quitter.

I am going to make it because You infuse me with strength and fortitude.

You will turn the obstacles into a path for my feet to walk on.

Every tough road I walk on will be a place of triumph as I keep going forward with determination and looking at You for my answers and help.

I decree You have never let me down and You never will.

I have every reason to succeed as I stay on the path You have for me, Lord.

Everywhere I walk I will find prosperity, favor, and success because I will never give up or quit.

- DAY 14 -

LORD OF THE BREAKTHROUGH

Today is a day of breakthrough; expect it.

You are breaking out and breaking through, whether you see it yet or not.

God is breaking the mold of wrong thinking that kept you locked up and bound to previous seasons; old patterns are being broken, and your old mindset is breaking off.

Your breakthrough is here; you have stood strong through the storms and allowed Him to break you out of the hurts and disappointments of the past.

It's a new day, a new season, and it's your time; you will see it as it becomes visible.

His breaker anointing will shake every shackle loose in your life that has been holding you back from stepping into your destiny and God-given inheritance.

What you went through didn't break you so you can now expect a breakthrough.

Stand still and see the deliverance of the Lord.

Exodus 12:23

For the Lord will pass through to smite the Egyptians; and when He sees the blood on the lintel and on the two doorposts, the Lord will pass over the door and will not allow the destroyer to come in to your houses to smite you.

Deuteronomy 7:15

And the Lord will take away from you all sickness, and will put none of the evil diseases of Egypt, which you know, upon you; but will lay them upon all them that hate you.

Micah 2:13

The one who breaks open will come up before them, they will break out, pass through the gate, and go out by it, their king will pass before them, with the Lord at their head.

2 Samuel 5:20

So David came to Baal-perazim and defeated them there; and he said, "The Lord has broken through my enemies before me like the breakthrough of waters." Therefore he named that place Baal-perazim.

<u>Declaration</u>

I declare today is the day of the breakthrough for me.

I give You permission to change my mind and take me higher in You where I can recognize and receive the changes I need.

You have brought me through, Lord, and I give You praise and thanksgiving.

I don't take any credit for what You've done in the past and I know You can do it again, for me.

I receive all that You are doing and believe Your timing is the very best.

- DAY 15 -

PASSING THROUGH DEEP WATERS

What you are going through today is not your destination; you are simply traveling through.

Your present circumstances, finances or relationships can make it seem like the water is quickly rising and there's no one to rescue you.

Remember, you are only passing through and God will always rescue you!

Jesus stretched out His hand and rescued Peter when he thought he was going to drown.

Take a deep breath of faith, reach out, and take hold of the mighty hand of God; together you are passing safely through the deep, murky waters of uncertainty.

Like Moses, your journey with Him will always take you safely through to the other side of the Red Sea; the safe way to pass through.

When you are in the valley feeling depressed, remember that there cannot be mountaintops without valleys; the safe way is to pass through the wilderness.

Don't make permanent decisions during temporary storms.

Remember where He has brought you from and where you're going.

Exodus 14:21

Then Moses stretched out his hand over the sea; and the Lord swept the sea back by a strong east wind all night and turned the sea into dry land, so the waters were divided.

Isaiah 43:2-3a

When you pass through the waters, I will be with you; and though the rivers, they will not overflow you...for I am the Lord your God.

Acts 7:36

And by means of many wonders and miraculous signs, He led them out of Egypt, through the Red Sea, and through the wilderness for forty years.

<u>Declaration</u>

I declare that nothing is too difficult for You Lord because I trust Your way.

You have already taken care of the situation that troubles me; I will not drown.

I decree that I am simply passing through a place that You will help me break through as I focus on You.

I decree the waters will part and I will not begin to sink, get wet or smell like smoke.

I receive supernatural power, provision, and perseverance to pass through any trial that comes at me on my journey.

I believe in and receive the presence of God that helps me overcome and makes me pass through every opposition.

- DAY 16 -

BLESSINGS OVERFLOWING

Concentrate on counting your blessings and you'll have little time to count anything else.

God bestows His blessings without discrimination and they are totally dependent on Him.

His infinite generosity will always exceed all your wishes, dreams and desires.

When you look for blessings, you will find more than you asked for, a bountiful land flowing with milk and honey.

God wants you to use your blessings to overflow onto others.

When you care about helping others, God assumes responsibility for your needs.

You cannot out-give God.

He sets up a beautiful banquet table just for you in the midst of your enemies.

Deuteronomy 1:11

May the Lord, the God of your fathers, increase you a thousand-fold more than you are and bless you, just as He has promised you!

Proverbs 10:22

The blessing of the Lord, it makes rich, and he adds no sorrow with it.

Isaiah 44:3

For I will pour water upon him that is thirsty, and floods upon the dry ground: I will pour my spirit upon your descendants, and my blessing upon your offspring.

Romans 5:13

May the God of hope fill you with all joy and peace as you trust in Him, so that you may overflow with hope by the power of the Holy Spirit.

Declaration

Today I choose to live in the overflow of God's blessings.

I am blessed in the city; I am blessed in the field.

I am blessed in my down setting, blessed in my uprising.

I am blessed, socially, physically, mentally, and physiologically.

I am blessed emotionally and interpersonally.

I am blessed and every part of my life is blessed.

I speak into my day and download prosperity and success into my day.

I declare I will overflow onto others the unimaginable blessings that come to me from God.

I will give Him praise and honor for blessing me with His presence, prosperity, and peace.

- DAY 17 -

GOD HEARS YOUR PRAYERS

God makes it clear that your prayers are very important to Him.

He loves when you communicate with Him just as you would your closest friend, and promises to be there for you whenever you call on His name.

He hears and will respond if you take time to listen.

God will bring hope to your heart, peace to your soul, and strength to your life.

Even when you're at a loss for words and don't know what to pray, the Holy Spirit Himself speaks on your behalf.

He wants you to talk with Him about everything, from your smallest victories to your greatest fears and everything in between.

You have a direct line to God and He is available to talk to you anytime, day or night.

Tell Him how much you love Him, need Him and appreciate Him; give Him all your burdens and cares.

He hears your weeping, your requests, your praise, and your thanksgiving.

Prayer moves God, and God moves mountains.

Jeremiah 29:13

Then you will call upon Me and come and pray to Me, and I will listen to you. You will seek Me and find Me when you search for Me with all your heart.

Psalm 34:4, 6

I sought the Lord, and He answered me, and delivered me from all my fears. This poor man cried, and the Lord heard him and saved him out of all his troubles.

Acts 10:31

Cornelius, God has heard your prayer and remembered your gifts to the poor.

<u>Declaration</u>

I praise You and thank You for hearing me when I cry out to You.

I believe You have taken care of everything that concerns me and I love being able to talk to You about all of it.

Thank You for sending the Holy Spirit who speaks for me when I am at a loss for words.

I declare the communication between You and me, God, is open and clear. I speak and You listen; You speak and I listen.

What a wonderful gift You have given me, Lord, an attentive, listening ear.

When no one else seems to listen or care, You always do.

I decree and believe You will always answer me when I call unto You in times of distress or confusion; You are always my answer.

HIS JOY IS YOUR STRENGTH

The Joy of the Lord is the gladness in your heart that comes from knowing Him.

Joy is a fruit of the Spirit, and it is your duty and privilege to rejoice in the Lord.

Today you can choose to rely on His Joy to be your strength.

As you face this day, don't face it on your own because you alone have limitations and your strength can fail you.

It is the Lord's joy that is your strength; His rejoicing that gives reason to rejoice; His joy that fills you with hope and His joyous wish to save you just as you are.

You can do everything you need to do today as you receive His strength.

Rely on the promise of His Word: "You infuse me with inner strength." Even when your strength seems limited and you find yourself feeling weak, He gives you His.

Today God is infusing you with inner joy and inner strength that does not come from you but from the unlimited resources of Heaven.

God never says, "I told you so," or, "You should have known better," or, "Look what a mess your life is in."

He is always with you and for you to give you His mighty supernatural strength as you remember to partner Him with joy and thanksgiving.

Praise Him now and get ready for a season of great gratitude and joy.

Psalm 28:7

The Lord is my strength and my shield; my heart trusts in Him, and He helps me. My heart leaps for joy, and with my song I praise Him.

Isaiah 40:29

He gives strength to the weary and increases the power of the weak.

Philippians 4:13

I can do all this through Him who gives me strength.

<u>Declaration</u>

I am ready to receive a season of great joy and great strength as You lift off of me every burden, concern, and care.

I declare that there are no limits to Your strength.

Thank You that You are infusing me with inner strength today, I believe it and receive it by faith.

I declare that I am strong in the Lord and the power of His might.

I decree that, even though I might feel weak at times, in You I am always strong.

I will believe Your Word, Father, and will not be led by any inadequate, intimidating or insecure feelings.

Thank You for Your supernatural joy and strength, Lord.

- DAY 19 -

FEAR NOT

Faith enables you to obey God without fear.

Give the fear of man over to God in prayer.

When you pray and believe, according to 1 John 5:14,15, God hears your prayers, grants your petitions and delivers you from all your fears.

Thank God throughout your day for setting you free from the bondage of fear.

Your salvation includes being saved, healed, protected, made whole, doing well, delivered and preserved because of what Jesus Christ did for you on the cross.

Boldly declare the covenant promises of God that defeated fear in your life.

No one was born fearful, you simply learned it on your journey; now it is your responsibility to re-learn His ways with new mindsets of faith.

When you move beyond fear, you are made free!

Psalm 34:4

I sought the Lord, and He answered me, and delivered me from all my fears.

Isaiah 54:17

No weapon that is formed against you shall prosper; and every tongue that shall rise against you in judgment you shall condemn. This is the heritage of the servants of the Lord, and their righteousness is of Me, says the Lord.

Philippians 4:6-7

Be careful (anxious) for nothing; but in everything by prayer and supplication with thanksgiving let your requests be made known unto God. And the peace of God, which passes all understanding, shall keep your hearts and minds through Christ Jesus.

Declaration

I declare I will not allow fear to hold me back.

I declare I will not allow fear to stop me from God's will coming to pass in my life.

I declare I will not allow fear to rule over my emotions but will be strong in the power of my faith in Jesus Christ.

Fear will bow to faith and no longer bind my mind with untrue thoughts.

My friends and family will see the significant change in me as I recognize and repent at how I used to allow fear to control me.

My faith will not be hindered by fear from creating new mindsets and new miracles ordained by the Lord.

HEARING GOD'S VOICE

God wants to fellowship and communicate with you more than anything else.

You can't really have a relationship unless there is true dialogue; talking and listening.

He talks; you listen. You talk; He listens.

God will speak to you through the Word, through your pastor or spiritual mentor, or through any method He chooses.

His voice will bring peace, correction, direction, wisdom, love, encouragement, and answers.

His voice never contradicts His Word, brings shame, discouragement or condemnation.

Obedience is the response that keeps the heart free of guilt and the communication with God wide open.

Past offenses can cause you to hear incorrectly; let them go.

If you refuse to do what God tells you in the little things, you risk deafening your spiritual ear.

Jesus never listened to a stranger's voice; He knew the voice of His Father.

Exodus 19:19

When the sound of the trumpet grew louder and louder, Moses spoke and God answered him with thunder.

Deuteronomy 13:4

You shall walk after the Lord your God, and fear Him, keep His commandments, obey His voice, and you shall serve Him, and cleave unto Him.

John 10:27

My sheep hear My voice, and I know them, and they follow (obey) Me.

Declaration

I declare and receive a new heart and new mind that hear God's voice correctly and clearly.

I repent of the hurts of the past that have interfered and clouded my hearing of God's voice.

I declare the voices of the past will no longer be louder than God's voice.

I will seek and know the Lord's voice above all other voices.

His voice is all that matters and I declare a heart after God that heeds His instructions.

I will hear with spiritual ears, a pure heart, a sound mind and agree with His voice above all others.

- DAY 21 -

DEVELOPING A MIRACLE MINDSET

You are just one thought away from your miracle.

Warning: your thoughts can run your life, make sure they line up with God's thoughts.

You are transformed by the renewing of your mind and the washing by the water of His Word.

Attitudes are governed by mindsets.

Never let your external thoughts dictate your internal atmosphere.

Wrong thoughts are strongholds that will keep you bound to untruths.

Take captive every thought that does not line up with the Word; cast them down immediately.

The carnal reasoning of the minds of natural men works against God and His spiritual plans.

A victim mentality will keep you from being a victor; let it go.

Forgiveness is a key to a healthy mind and heart.

Proverbs 4:23

Be very careful about what you think. Your thoughts run your life.

Proverbs 23:7

For as he thinks in his heart, so is he.

Romans 15:6

That you may with one mind and one mouth glorify God, even the Father of our Lord Jesus Christ.

2 Corinthians 10:5

Casting down imaginations, and every high thing that exalts itself against the knowledge of God, and bringing into captivity every thought to the obedience of Christ.

<u>Declaration</u>

I declare my attitude is governed by my new mind-set.

I declare I will not allow any carnal thoughts to dictate my spiritual atmosphere.

I declare a new heart and mind belongs to me because of the blood of Jesus that set me free from Adam's disobedience and the curse.

I receive a changed, renewed mind, which causes me to be in unity with the mind and body of Christ.

I will not allow any wrong thinking to stop me from receiving my miracle today.

Thank You that I am being transformed by the renewing of my mind and the washing by the water of Your Word; I receive my brand new, pure mind, Lord.

GOD IS FOR YOU

Since God is for you, nothing or no one can successfully ever be against you.

There are plenty of opposing forces against you but nothing can successfully overthrow you.

God is for you and gave you His Son as a sacrifice once and for all for your sins.

God is for you and gave you His Holy Spirit to be your guide, comforter, and teacher.

God is for you and adopted you into His family as a joint heir with His Son.

God is for you and promised to work all things for your good.

God is for you and guaranteed your eternal security with Him in Heaven.

Psalm 139:15

My frame was not hidden from you when I was made in the secret place, when I was woven together in the depths of the earth.

Romans 8:28

And we know that all things work together for good to them that love God, to them who are the called according to His purpose.

Romans 8:31

What, then, shall we say in response to these things? If God is for us, who can be against us?

Declaration

I declare that, since my God is for me today, nothing can be against me!

I decree that, since my God is for me, His promises are for my family and me; He is on our side.

I receive all that God has planned for me as an adopted child in the household of faith.

By faith I know that God is on my side and He fights all battles on my behalf; all I have to do is believe, obey and trust Him.

Thank You, Lord, for Your Son Jesus who completed my atonement and sits at the right hand of our Father interceding for me right now.

I declare that You and I are the winning team, even though it sometimes looks like no one else is on my side.

I am overflowing with gratitude and thanksgiving today that You will never leave me.

- DAY 23 -

YOUR FOUNDATION OF FAITH

Faith does not work with tradition and customs.

Tradition says, "This is how it has always been done," while faith says, "This is how God wants it done now."

Your faith may not make everything easy but will always make things possible.

Faith is acting on what you believe.

Faith overcomes powerful opposition by focusing on the unseen God.

Faith produces what you want; trust produces what God wants.

A dangerous person you should always keep out of your life is the one who feeds your doubts and weakens your faith.

"Faith expects from God what is beyond all expectation." ~ Andrew Murray

Nothing is too difficult for Him.

Psalm 94:14

For the Lord will not abandon His people, nor will He forsake His inheritance.

Hebrews 11:1-3

Now faith is confidence in what we hope for and assurance about what we do not see. This is what the ancients were commended for. By faith we understand that the universe was formed at God's command, so that what is seen was not made out of what was visible.

2 Corinthians 5:7

For we live by faith and not by sight.

<u>Declaration</u>

I declare the one true living God, the Father of all creation, was manifested in the flesh for my salvation and that of all mankind who believes.

I declare that the Spirit dwells in the heart of every man who believes and is baptized in Your name.

I decree His name, the name above every other name, is JESUS CHRIST.

My faith will arise and overpower fear.

I will believe the Word of God and not what my present circumstances might be saying; He will not forsake me.

There is nothing my faith cannot accomplish according to His perfect will.

My faith is more powerful than anyone's doubts.

My faith in Jesus will teach my mouth to speak in agreement with what I believe.

I am living by faith and not by sight, in Jesus' mighty name.

- DAY 24 -

GOD DELIGHTS IN YOUR PROSPERITY

If God is going to bless someone today, it might as well be you.

He delights in your prosperity and His blessings are yours today.

The guidelines in the Word for achieving true prosperity are eternal.

Money is a tool to help you do what's really important, which is serving Him and His children.

Being prosperous not only means having wealth, but health, happiness, long life, and success; God promises all these to you in His Word.

Joseph was prosperous and successful because the Lord was with him.

Joseph may have been "a slave that owned nothing" in the eyes of the world but God blessed Potiphar's household with influence and prosperity because Joseph was serving there.

Because Joseph was a faithful servant of God, whatever he did to please God blessed and prospered whoever was around him.

Jesus died and was resurrected for you so you could not only have forgiveness of sins and eternal life, but also wealth, success, and prosperity.

Prosperity is the favor with God and man. When you know who you are in Christ, and when you have enough to do what He has called you to do, that is when you move into the place of being content with what you have.

God's plans for your life include prosperity and never poverty, and His plans to bless you are meant to bring glory to Himself.

Genesis 39:2-3

And the Lord was with Joseph, and he was a prosperous man; and he was in the house of his master the Egyptian. And his master saw that the Lord was with him, and that the Lord made all that he did to prosper in his hand.

Deuteronomy 28:11

*The L*ORD *will grant you abundant prosperity—in the fruit of your womb, the young of your livestock and the crops of your ground—in the land He swore to your ancestors to give you.*

3 John 1:2

Beloved, I wish above all things that you may prosper and be in health, even as your soul prospers.

<u>Declaration</u>

I declare and decree that wealth and riches of God are in my house right now.

I partner with the Lord for His success, prosperity, health, and abundance of joy.

My family and those around me will continuously be blessed as I continue to live in obedience and favor with God and man.

I expect to see an increase come to my household as I praise You in all things.

YOUR PLACE OF REFUGE

God alone is your refuge when anxiety, insecurity, and uncertainty try to force you to quit, and death, disease, and debt try to make you run and hide.

His secret place of refuge provides your spirit with a never-ending shelter to run to.

There is no storm that is so powerful it will overtake you if you remember to take refuge in Him.

He is your continual safety net and hiding place.

Watch the destruction pass by from your peaceful place of refuge.

He is your permanent shelter to run to when you have any kind of need.

Psalm 46:1

God is our refuge and strength, a very present help in times of trouble.

Psalm 32:7

David says this of God, "You are my hiding place; You preserve me from trouble; You surround me with songs of deliverance."

Psalm 91:4

He will cover you with his feathers, and under His wings you will find refuge; His faithfulness will be your shield and rampart.

Proverbs 14:26

In the fear of the Lord is strong confidence: and His children shall have a place of refuge.

Declaration

I declare my God is my refuge and I can go and hide in Him.

I declare my God is my shelter from every dangerous storm.

I declare my God is my hiding place where I will never be afraid, moved or left alone.

I declare my God is my place of escape into the Spirit where the carnality of the world cannot tempt me or touch me.

I will run to You, Lord, and will not be shaken with fear, anxiety or stress.

I will remember that I always have a safe place in You.

EMBRACE THE PROCESS

The process prepares you for the promise.

People want the promise but often choose to abort the process.

Without God's process, you have no real destiny in Him and it becomes all about you.

Embrace His process as He leads you into your promised land.

There is a beautiful promise waiting for you on the other side of the process.

The prodigal son ran from the process but changed his mind and returned.

If you have wandered from the process you can repent, return and get back on track right now.

Don't redecorate and camp out in the wilderness, you were meant for Canaan.

The pressure has been building and suddenly it will burst forth.

Learn lessons during the process.

Don't worry about the cost of the process; it has already been paid in full.

Your miracle will manifest when you choose to embrace the process.

If you demand a particular process, you will miss out on the very circumstances God planned and provided in order to shape you into His image.

If you embrace His process, especially when it doesn't make sense, He will take good care of you and the outcome.

Embrace the process and He will get you where He wants you in order to protect you and prosper you.

Exodus 13:21

And the Lord went before them by day in a pillar of a cloud, to lead them in the way; and by night in a pillar of fire, to give them light; to go by day and night.

Acts 27:24

And said, 'Do not be afraid, Paul; you must stand before Caesar. And look, God has granted you the lives of all who sail with you.'

2 Timothy 2:9

For which I suffer to the extent of being chained like a criminal. But the Word of God cannot be chained!

<u>Declaration</u>

I declare I will let go and embrace the process because I trust You, Lord.

I declare I am free of controlling fear and submit to Your power to take me through to where I need to be.

I decree Your Wisdom overtakes me and directs me on the path which You have prepared for me.

I will believe, listen, rest and embrace Your still small voice that says, "This is the way, walk in it."

YOUR HOPE IS IN GOD

Your circumstances may make you feel completely discouraged but your hope is in the Lord.

What you are facing may look overwhelming, but your hope is always in God.

The present situation may be too difficult for you to figure out, but in Christ alone is where your hope is.

No matter what is going on in your life, you can trust that He is in control to work everything out for your good.

He has done it for you before and He will do it again.

God knows intimately every concern of your heart and has planned a route of escape.

If you give up all hope, you give up on the miracle. Your hope is in Him!

Jeremiah 29:11

'For I know the plans I have for you,' says the Lord. 'They are plans for good and not for evil, to give you a future and a hope.'

Psalm 39:7

And now, Lord, what do I wait for? My hope is in You.

Romans 15:13

Now the God of hope fills you with all joy and peace in believing, that you may abound in hope, through the power of the Holy Spirit.

<u>Declaration</u>

I declare that my hope will not be in an earthly person, a place or position.

My hope will not be in what I can figure out or see in the natural.

My hope will always be in the Lord.

You will never leave my family or me alone, and I am thankful that You know exactly what we are facing.

My hope is in You, for You will always see me through to the miracle.

You have planned only good for my life and my future.

I declare that nothing is too difficult for You.

There is light at the end of every tunnel I walk through; His name is Jesus.

I decree the ending of turmoil is coming into focus as my eyes are fixed on You.

My hope is in the Lord.

TRUST THE LORD

Trust God today; the biggest rewards always carry the biggest risks.

Trust means a firm belief in the reliability, truth, ability or strength of someone or something, and confidence, belief, faith, certainty, assurance, and conviction.

When you realize you are beginning to fight the situation, switch back to trust again.

Trust is often called "surrender".

Trust is often called "submission".

Trust looks like faith.

Trust feels like letting go of all concerns, worries or anxieties.

Trust Him with your family, your future, your finances, your health and everything that concerns you.

Psalm 9:10

Those who know Your name trust in You, for You, O Lord, do not abandon those who search for you.

Proverbs 3:5-6

Trust in the Lord with all your heart and lean not on your own understanding; in all your ways submit to Him, and He will make your paths straight.

Romans 15:13

May the God of hope fill you with all joy and peace as you trust in Him, so that you may overflow with hope by the power of the Holy Spirit.

Declaration

I trust You with all that I am and all that I have.

There is nothing I don't have that You didn't give me; so it all belongs to You.

I declare I will not rely on what I see, hear or understand from this earthly realm.

I declare I will only trust in what I hear, see and understand from the Spirit.

I trust in Your provision, Your healing power, Your faithful love and Your infinite wisdom today.

As I surrender today, there is nothing I cannot trust You with, Lord.

BE YOURSELF

BE YOU—God has a specific race for you to run.

It's not how you start the race but how you finish; no one can do it but you.

You are equipped, qualified and called to be an original.

You are God's first choice.

You are perfectly created to be what God created you to be.

Don't try to wear or walk inside someone else's shoes.

There is a uniqueness that God has placed inside of you that only you carry.

You can believe, belong and become everything He promised you.

See yourself through God's eyes and not through the eyes of those who don't recognize or highly value your worth.

Be you—He loves everything about you.

Psalm 139:13-14

For You formed my inmost being; You knit me together in my mother's womb. I praise You because I am fearfully and wonderfully made; Your works are wonderful, I know that full well.

Isaiah 44:24

Thus says the Lord, your Redeemer, and the one who formed you from the womb, "I, the Lord, am the maker of all things, stretching out the heavens by Myself and spreading out the earth all alone."

Ephesians 1:3-4

Blessed be the God and Father of our Lord Jesus Christ, who has blessed us in Christ with every spiritual blessing in the heavenly places, even as He chose us in Him before the foundation of the world, that we should be holy and blameless before Him.

1 Peter 2:9

You are a chosen race, a royal priesthood, a holy nation, a people for His own possession, that you may proclaim the excellencies of Him who called you out of darkness into His marvelous light.

Declaration

I declare I will be me, the one God made an original treasure unto Himself.

Today, I am reminding myself of my unique qualities He chose to bless the world with.

I decree I will not try to be something or someone I am not; I will be like Jesus.

I am God's first choice to do what He's called me to do; this is my confidence, which is in Him.

I bless You, Lord, for making me into Your image and likeness; I give You praise for You do all things beautifully and do not make mistakes.

- DAY 30 -

NEVER ALONE

You are not alone, even though the road may seem dark and lonely.

You may feel like your whole world is turned upside down, but you are not alone.

God is right there beside you and will never abandon you.

He has given you the Comforter to teach you, and ministering angels to protect you. He calls that your very own personal entourage.

He will never leave you; for, wherever you are, God is there.

He knows where you are at all times and He knows exactly what you're going through; you are never alone.

God never loses sight of you and never wonders what to do for you.

His plans for your safety and welfare will always work out; you are never alone.

Joshua 1:9

Have I not commanded you? Be strong and courageous. Do not be frightened, and do not be dismayed, for the LORD your God is with you wherever you go.

Isaiah 43:5

Do not fear, for I am with you; I will bring your offspring from the east, and gather you from the west.

Matthew 28:20

Teaching them to observe all that I have commanded you. And behold, I am with you always, to the end of the age.

Hebrews 13:5c

For He Himself has said, I will never leave you or forsake you.

Declaration

Thank You, Lord, for Your promises to be with me always; You are truth and cannot lie.

I declare I am full of the Spirit of God and will never be left alone.

I am reminded continuously that when I am feeling abandoned, You are there.

I decree the promises of God are "Yes" and "Amen"; He is the Word of Truth.

I am surrounded by Your love, the greatest power in the universe; how can I ever feel alone again?

I give You praise for all that I need is in You and You are with me forever.

- DAY 31 -

YOUR FUTURE IS BRIGHT AND YOUR DESTINY IS SURE

Agreement with your future accelerates the fulfillment of your destiny.

Agreement with God's plan for your life provides a clear and imminent revelation of your future.

You can't start the next chapter of your life if you keep re-reading the last one.

God has already seen your future and prepared everything in it for you. Don't look back; look forward.

You are not defined by your past; God has a beautiful future for you and it begins here, and it starts now.

A continual heart of gratitude will propel you into your destiny.

There's a reason your windshield is bigger than your rear view mirror; where you're headed is more important than where you've been.

You will never get to where you want to be until you let go of where you've been; you are only one person away from your next season.

Something incredible is being produced; the power of the resurrection followed the obedience of the crucifixion.

Keep your words in agreement with His dreams for you because fear and doubt can stop you from moving forward.

The promotion follows adversity so keep your eyes on the bigger picture.

Goliath was created to help David become who he was appointed to be; don't be moved by the opposition, just keep your eyes on the Promised Land.

Your future is unlike any yesterday you have ever known; press toward the destiny He's shown you.

"You can't go back and change the beginning but you can start where you are and change the ending."
~ CS Lewis

Jeremiah 29:11

For I know the plans I have for you, says the Lord. They are plans for good and not for evil, to give you a future and a hope.

Isaiah 43:18

Forget the former things, do not dwell on the past.

I Corinthians 2:9

But as it is written, "No eye has seen, no ear has heard, and no mind has imagined the things that God has prepared for those who love Him."

<u>Declaration</u>

I declare my destiny is shining brightly into my unimaginable future full of abundance, authority, power, and love.

I receive the future outcome built on hope and joy as I put my trust in You, Lord.

I decree I will continue to build and walk on the sure foundation of Your Word.

– In Conclusion –

Deuteronomy 28:1-14

If you fully obey the Lord your God and carefully follow all his commands I give you today, the Lord your God will set you high above all the nations on earth. All these blessings will come on you and accompany you if you obey the Lord your God: You will be blessed in the city and blessed in the country. The fruit of your womb will be blessed, and the crops of your land and the young of your livestock—the calves of your herds and the lambs of your flocks. Your basket and your kneading trough will be blessed. You will be blessed when you come in and blessed when you go out. The Lord will grant that the enemies who rise up against you will be defeated before you. They will come at you from one direction but flee from you in seven. The Lord will send a blessing on your barns and on everything you put your hand to. The Lord your God will bless you in the land He is giving you. The Lord will establish you as His holy people, as He promised you on oath, if you keep the commands of the LORD your God and walk in obedience to Him. Then all the peoples on earth will see that you are called by the name of the LORD, and they will fear you. The LORD will grant you abundant prosperity—in the fruit of your womb, the young of your livestock and the crops of your ground—in the land He swore to your ancestors to give you. The LORD will open the heavens, the storehouse of His bounty, to send rain on your land in season and to bless all the work of your hands. You will lend to many nations but will borrow from none. The LORD will make you the head, not the tail. If you pay attention to the commands of the LORD your God that I give you this day and carefully follow them, you will always be at the top, never at the bottom. Do not turn aside from any of the commands I give you today, to the right or to the left, following other gods and serving them.

Declaration

I speak salvation over my household and those close to me.

I release prosperity and success to those I love.

I declare that our lives are coming into alignment with Heaven and all that is stored up for us there.

I speak to my government that they will lead our country both morally and ethically.

I speak peace into my mind and courage into my heart to be led by the Spirit and not by sight or emotions.

I speak into my feet that there are paths I can walk to overcome every obstacle.

I am the head and not the tail, the first and not the last, above and not beneath.

I am loved by God, chosen by God, and protected by the one true living God.

Every good and perfect gift comes from above.

This day is my gift, therefore it will begin perfect, and it will end powerfully good, in Jesus' mighty name.

Meet the Authors

Joe and Bella Garcia have been happily married for 27 years and have three children; Andrew, Joel, and Rachel. They are business owners, revivalists and lead pastors at The River International Church, an apostolic center based in Hamilton, Ontario, Canada. They have ministered in many nations of the world, including Mozambique, Brazil, Trinidad and Tobago, the USA, Portugal, Bulgaria and Sri Lanka. Their passion is for the equipping of the saints, to raise up leaders, and to see them established and released into their God-given destiny. They carry a breaker anointing, a revival spirit, and they move in the prophetic. Their passion is to pursue the presence of God, and, as they make room for Him in their meetings, God moves with miracles, signs, and wonders for the people.

Dear Reader,

If your life was touched while reading *Igniting Your Day please* let us know! We would love to celebrate with you! Please visit our website, www.theriverin-you.com

Spreading Glory Fires from the River to the Ends of the Earth,

Pastors Joe and Bella Garcia

 Facebook: Joe Garcia , Bella Garcia

 Instagram: pjgarcia & bellag777

 Twitter: @pjgarcia7 & bgarcia777

"A presence-driven publisher making your book dream come true!"

CONTACT INFO

Joe & Bella Garcia at

info@glorycarriersinternational.com

88551345R00059

Made in the USA
Columbia, SC
07 February 2018